This copy of

THE EVEN SMELLIER SOCKS
JOKE BOOK

belongs to

Andrew Walters

THE EVEN SMELLIER SOCKS

Karen King

Cover and illustrations by
Andrew Warrington

RED FOX

A Red Fox Book

Published by Random House Children's Books
20 Vauxhall Bridge Road, London SW1V 2SA

A division of Random House UK Ltd
London Melbourne Sydney Auckland
Johannesburg and agencies throughout the world

Typeset by SX Composing DTP, Rayleigh, Essex
Printed and bound in Great Britain by
Cox & Wyman Limited, Reading, Berkshire

Papers used by Random House UK Limited are natural,
recyclable products made from wood grown in sustainable
forests. The manufacturing processes conform to the
environmental regulations of the country of origin.

RANDOM HOUSE UK Limited Reg No. 954009

ISBN 0 09 926513 3

CONTENTS

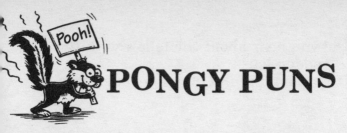

PONGY PUNS

Where does a swallow live?
In a throat.

What are sideburns?
What you get when your electric blanket is too hot.

What's the one advantage of being bald?
You can style your hair with a damp cloth.

What does every winner lose in a race?
His breath.

FRED: I'm so thirsty my tongue is hanging out.
MARY: So that's what it is – I thought it was your tie!

What do you lose each time you stand up?
Your lap.

Did you hear about the fellow with the
   wooden leg?
It went on fire and burnt to the ground.

SUE: What happened to your wavy hair?
MANDY: It waved goodbye.

TOM: Why is your arm in a sling?
SAM: Because I seem to get all the breaks.

STEVE: Why are your hands shaking?
MARK: They're pleased to see each other.

CUSTOMER: Do you have pigs' feet?
BUTCHER: Yes, I do.
CUSTOMER: I thought you were walking
   funny.

What happened to the lady who ate a
   lump of sugar?
She got a lump in her throat.

There was once a little boy with a turned-
   up nose.
*Every time he breathed out he blew his
   cap off.*

Did you hear about the man who was so
short-sighted he couldn't get to sleep
unless he counted elephants?

VAIN GIRL: My boyfriend says I have skin
   like a peach.
CHEEKY LITTLE BROTHER: Who wants to
   look like a nineteen-year-old peach?

What trees do fingers and thumbs grow
   on?
Palm trees.

What tongue never speaks?
The tongue in your shoes.

What do you call a very small mother?
A minimum!

MUM (to little boy): Ben, you've been
  fighting again and lost two of your
  teeth!
BEN: I haven't lost them, Mum, they're in
  my pocket.

Why did the man comb his hair with his
  toes?
To make ends meet.

How do you define agony?
A one-armed man with an itchy bum
hanging from a cliff-top.

GRANNY: Richard, why is your face so red?
RICHARD: I was running to stop a fight.
GRANNY: That was very good of you. Who was fighting?
RICHARD: Me and another boy.

FAT LADY (getting off bus): This bus was very slow.
CONDUCTOR: It'll pick up now you're getting off.

WHAT A STINK!

GIRL: My sister uses lemon juice for her complexion.
FRIEND: No wonder she always looks so sour.

FATHER: Eat your spinach, Emily, it'll put colour in your cheeks.
EMILY: But, Daddy, I don't want green cheeks!

What does a thirsty foot do?
Put on tap shoes.

What did the finger say to the thumb?
People will say we're in glove.

Why did the lady have her hair in a bun?
*Because she had her nose in a
cheeseburger.*

DAD: Who gave you that black eye?
DANNY: No one gave it to me, Dad. I had
to fight for it.

TINA: My baby brother's only a year old
and he's been walking for six months.
ANNIE: Really, he must be very tired.

Knock, knock.
Who's there?
Rupert who?
Rupert your left arm in, your left arm
    out . . .

Why do people laugh up their sleeves?
Because that's where their funny-bone is.

My wife is like the Mona Lisa.
*You mean she's beautiful with a
    mysterious smile?*
No, she's as flat as a canvas and ought to
    be in a museum.

Why did the old-age pensioner put wheels
    on his rocking chair?
Because he wanted to rock and roll.

MUM: Jimmy, pick your feet up when you
    walk!
JIMMY: But, Mum, I'll only have to put
    them down again.

Who was that at the door?
A chap with a wooden leg.
Tell him to hop it!

Why are tall people lazier than short
   people?
Because they're longer in bed.

JENNY: I haven't slept for days.
SARAH: Why not?
JENNY: I sleep at night.

Did you hear about the cross-eyed
   teacher?
He had no control over his pupils.

SCHOOL NURSE: Have your eyes been
   checked lately?
PUPIL: No, they've always been plain blue
   with a black dot in the middle.

Why did the dishonest man grow a beard?
So no one could call him a bare-faced liar.

What happened when the
   idiot had a brain transplant?
The brain rejected him.

When are broken bones useful?
When they start to knit.

What do you call a man with a bus on his
　　head?
Dead.

When are eyes not eyes?
When the wind makes them water.

What country has no fat people?
Finland.

Why are feet like ancient tales?
Because they are leg-ends.

What does a deaf fisherman need?
A herring-aid.

MUM: Did you get a haircut, Billy?
BILLY: No, Mum, I got all of them cut.

SID: My brother was arrested for flat feet.
ANDY: Why's that?
SID: They were in the wrong flat.

Mummy, Mummy, can I lick out the bowl?
No. You'll flush the toilet like everybody else.

Knock, knock.
Who's there?
Ammonia.
Ammonia who?
Ammonia little girl and I can't reach the
  door.

What do you call a woman with one leg
  shorter than the other?
Eileen.

Knock, knock.
Who's there?
Dan.
Dan who?
Dan Druff.

What are long, pointed and run in families?
Noses.

Did you hear about the man who kept his
 wife under the bed?
He thought she was a little potty!

Knock, knock.
Who's there?
Anita.
Anita who?
Anita go to the loo.

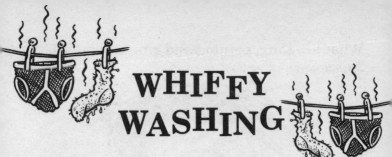

WHIFFY WASHING

What jacket is always burning?
A blazer.

What gloves can you hold but not wear?
Foxgloves.

What coat do you put on only when it's wet?
A coat of paint.

Who makes suits and eats spinach?
Popeye the Tailorman.

What do you get if you cross a shirt with a piece of jewellery?
A ring around the collar.

What do all women look for but hope never to find?
Holes in their tights.

Why do robbers wear braces?
Because they're hold-up men.

What's the best way to make a pair of
  trousers last?
Wear the jacket first.

What gets wetter the more it dries?
A towel.

A fellow called Fred didn't care
What kind of clothes he'd wear.
His jacket was raggy,
His trousers were baggy,
And that's why folk called him Fred Bare.

LADY: Do you like this dress? It's seventy years old.
LITTLE BOY: Did you make it yourself?

Why did the golfer wear an extra pair of trousers?
In case he got a hole in one.

A man went swimming and all his clothes were stolen, so what did he come home in?
The dark.

When do swimming trunks go ding dong?
When you wring them out.

MOTHER: Ben! Have you fallen over in your new trousers?
BEN: Yes, Mum. I didn't have time to take them off.

SUSIE: Last week a man stole a trolley of food and a pair of trousers from my uncle's supermarket.
AMY: Did your uncle chase him?
SUSIE: No, they were his trousers.

20

What does a boy do when he wears his trousers out?
Wears them in again.

What runs around all day and lies about at night with its tongue hanging out?
A pair of trainers.

If a crocodile skin makes a pair of shoes what do you make from banana skins?
Slippers.

MAN IN CLOTHES SHOP: I'd like some tight jeans.
SHOP ASSISTANT: Certainly sir. Will you walk this way?
MAN: If they're as tight as yours I'll probably have to.

What dress does everyone have but nobody wears?
An address.

LADY: Will this squirrel-hair coat be all right in the rain?
SHOP ASSISTANT: Of course. Have you ever seen a squirrel with an umbrella?

To whom do people always take off their hats?
Hairdressers.

AMY: I choose my own clothes.
ZOE: It seems to be a moth that chews mine.

What is always dressing?
Salad cream.

What did the shirt say to the trousers?
Meet me on the clothes-line – that's where I hang out.

What wears a coat all winter and pants all summer?
A dog.

Why is a tight shoe like fine summer weather?
They both make corn grow.

What coat has the most sleeves?
A coat of arms.

MOTHER: Why are you wearing your socks inside out, Jimmy?

JIMMY: Because there are holes in the other side.

Did you hear about the man who threw away his shoes because they were sticking their tongues out at him?

Rubber gloves are things you can put on, then wash your hands without getting them wet.

Donald and Ronald were two dim-witted removal men. One day, Donald was struggling to lift a large wardrobe up the front steps of the house.

'Why don't you get Ronald to help you?' asked the driver.

'He's inside, carrying the clothes,' said Donald.

An elderly aunt wanted to send her niece a coat for her birthday. The niece lived at the other end of country so the aunt had to post it and was worried about the cost. She put a note in the pocket saying, 'Dear Jenny, here is a new coat for you. I've taken off the brass buttons so it doesn't cost so much to post. You'll find them in the left-hand pocket of the coat. Love from Aunt Maud.'

Why do we buy clothes?
Because we can't get them for nothing.

Why do footballers wear shorts?
They'd be arrested if they didn't.

Why did the idiot spring out of the window?
To try his new jump suit.

LADY: Do you sell crocodile shoes?
SHOP ASSISTANT: How big is your crocodile, madam?

What's blue and wears a red scarf?
A freezing snowman.

Why did the fireman wear red trousers?
His blue ones were at the cleaners.

Knock, knock.
Who's there?
Pyjamas.
Pyjamas who?
Pyjamas round me honey, hold me tight . . .

A sheriff rode into town one day and asked the people if they'd seen a cowboy wearing a paper hat and shirt.

'No,' said a man. 'What's he wanted for?'

'Rustlin',' said the sheriff.

In which tree would you hang up your
    underwear?
In a pantry – or a vestry.

Where does a frog hang its overcoat?
In the croakroom.

What did the hat say to the scarf?
I'll go on ahead, you hang around.

SHERLOCK HOLMES: Ah. Watson, you're
    wearing your red thermal underwear.
DR WATSON: Absolutely amazing, Holmes.
    How did you deduce that?
HOLMES: Elementary, my dear Watson!
    You've forgotten to put your trousers
    on again!

What kind of clothing could you make
    from tea bags?
A baggy T-shirt.

Knock, knock.
Who's there?
Bella.
Bella who?
Bella bottom trousers.

Where does Tarzan
   buy his clothes?
At a jungle sale.

MAN: Have you any blue ties to match my
   eyes?
SHOP ASSISTANT: No, but we've got some
   soft hats to match your head.

What do lawyers wear in court?
Law suits.

What kind of pump can you eat?
A pumpkin.

What wears shoes but has no feet?
A pavement.

Did you hear about the boy who turned
   up at school with only one glove on?
The teacher asked him why and he
replied, 'Well the weather man said it
might be warm, but on the other hand it
might be cool.'

Did you hear about the man who put on a
   clean pair of socks every day?
By the end of the week he couldn't get his
shoes on.

GUEST: Are the sheets clean?
HOTELIER: Of course they're clean. I only
   washed them this morning. If you don't
   believe me have a feel; they're still
   damp.

Why is a small boy like a flannel?
Because they both shrink from washing.

Why do businessmen always carry
   umbrellas?
Because umbrellas can't walk.

Lost: school scarf by small boy with green and blue stripes.

What's the best way to cover a cushion?
Sit on it.

CUSTOMER: I'd like a dress to match my eyes, please.
SHOP ASSISTANT: Sorry, madam, we don't sell bloodshot dresses.

TEACHER: Polly, why are you wearing your earmuffs in the classroom?
POLLY: Because I'm trying to stop everything going in one ear and out of the other.

CUSTOMER: You've made this suit tighter than my skin.
TAILOR: Tighter than your skin? That's impossible!
CUSTOMER: Well, I can sit down in my skin but I can't in this suit.

FIRST MAN: Have you got holes in your socks?.
SECOND MAN: Certainly not!
FIRST MAN: How do you get your feet in them, then?

MOTHER: Jane, pull up your tights,
   they're all wrinkled.
JANE: But, Mum, I'm not wearing tights!

Why do judo experts wear black belts?
To keep their trousers up.

What did the police constable say to his
   belly button?
You're under a vest.

Why is the Antarctic always so cold?
It wears an ice cap.

What comes out of the North Sea and
   shouts 'Knickers'?
Crude oil.

What comes out of a plant and shouts
   'Lingerie'?
Refined oil.

BEASTLY BEASTS

What do duck decorators do?
Paper over the quacks.

How do you stop a herd of elephants from charging?
Take away their credit cards.

What's a frog spy called?
A croak and dagger agent.

What lion never attacks?
A dandelion.

Hey, diddle, diddle,
The cat played the fiddle,
The cow jumped over the moon,
The little dog laughed to see such fun,
But the farmer wasn't very pleased!

What's black, crazy and sits in a tree?
A raven lunatic.

How can you stop moles digging up your
   garden?
Hide the spade.

What did the mouse say when it lost its
   front teeth?
Hard cheese.

What bird lives down a coal pit?
A mynah bird.

Why does the owl make everyone laugh?
Because he's such a hoot.

What do polar bears have for lunch?
Iceburgers.

What do you call two spiders who have
    just got married?
Newly-webs.

How do you get rid of a white elephant?
Put it in a jumbo sale.

How can you tell which end of a worm is
    his head?
*Tickle his middle and see which end
    smiles.*

MANDY: I've just swallowed a long, fat
    worm.
ZOE: Shouldn't you take something for it?
MANDY: Certainly not. I'm going to let it
    starve.

What do animals read in zoos?
Gnus' papers.

How do you start a flea race?
One, two, flea, go!

Why did the elephant sit on the tomato?
He wanted to play squash.

Who went into the tiger's lair and came
out alive?
The tiger.

What happened to the snake with a cold?
She adder viper nose.

What do you get when you cross rabbits
with leeks?
Bunions.

Why can't you put an elephant in a sandwich?
Because he's too heavy to lift.

Where do you find giant snails?
On the end of giants' fingers.

What do you get if you sit under a cow?
A pat on the head.

What do you get if you cross an elephant with a box of laxative pills?
Out of the way.

Why did the two boa constrictors get married?
Because they had a crush on each other.

Where do insects live?
Crawley.

What's a sleeping bull called?
A bull dozer.

A man wanted to hire a horse, so he was told to ask the local priest. The priest agreed to hire him the horse but said that it only obeyed two commands – 'Alleluya!' to stop and 'Thank the Lord!' to go.

So the man set off on the horse, saying 'Thank the Lord, thank the Lord!'

The horse trotted faster and faster, then the man realised that they were approaching a cliff. 'Stop!' he shouted, but the horse carried on trotting.

They were right at the cliff edge when the man remembered the command to make the horse stop and yelled 'Alleluya!' The horse stopped at once.

The man breathed a sigh of relief and called out gratefully, 'Thank the Lord!'

What do you get if you cross an elephant with a skunk?
A big stinker.

What do you call a high-rise home for pigs?
A sty scraper.

What do you give a sick bird?
Tweetment.

How do you keep an elephant from
    smelling?
Tie a knot in its trunk.

How do fleas get from place to place?
By itch-hiking.

How do hippos play squash?
They jump on each other.

What is the smallest ant in the world?
An infant.

There were two flies in the airing
    cupboard. Which one was Scottish?
The one on the pipes.

How do chickens communicate?
By using fowl language.

Which airline do fleas fly on?
British Hairways.

How do you get down from an elephant?
You don't, you get down from a duck.

Why shouldn't you tell a secret to a pig?
Because they're squealers.

Why are four-legged animals such bad
   dancers?
They have two left feet.

Why do bees have sticky hair?
Because they have honey combs.

GAMEKEEPER: Have you ever hunted bear?
TOURIST: No, but I've gone fishing in my
  shorts.

Ding dong bell,
Pussy's in the well.
We've put some disinfectant down,
And that has cured the smell.

What do you get if you cross a galaxy with
  a toad?
Star warts.

What do you call a bee with a quiet buzz?
A mumble bee.

How do you spell 'mousetrap' using only
  three letters?
CAT.

What do you call a sheep
  with a machine gun?
Lambo.

What goes zzub zzub?
A bee flying backwards.

What animal drives a motor car?
A road hog.

Why did the fish blush?
It saw the ocean's bottom.

What do you get if you cross a cat with a chemist's?
Puss in Boots.

Why did the elephant wear sunglasses on the beach?
Because he didn't want to be recognised in the crowd.

Why aren't elephants allowed on the beach?
Their trunks might fall down.

When do mice need umbrellas?
When it's raining cats and dogs.

How does a monkey make toast?
He puts it under a gorilla.

Why did the cat eat cheese?
*So he could sit by a mousehole with baited
   breath.*

Why do birds in nests always stay friends?
Because they don't want to fall out.

What sort of fish can't swim?
A dead one.

Why do elephants have trunks?
*Because they'd look pretty stupid with
   suitcases.*

A curious beast is the monkey,
It might be thin or chunky,
If it has green hair,
And rings on its ears,
It must be a punky monkey.

A man was walking down the street when he saw a kangaroo. So he held it by the hand and took it to a policeman. 'I've just found this kangaroo, officer,' he said. 'What shall I do with it?"

'Take it to the zoo,' said the policeman.

The next day, the policeman saw the man walking down the street again with the kangaroo.

'I thought I told you to take that kangaroo to the zoo,' he said.

'I did,' said the man. 'And this afternoon I'm taking it to the pictures.'

What do you get if you cross a cow with a
    kangaroo?
I don't know, but you'd have to milk it on
    a pogo stick.

Knock, knock.
Who's there?
Goose.
Goose who?
Goose who's knocking at your door.

What do you call a happy gorilla?
A gayrilla.

Why do gorillas have big nostrils?
Have you seen the size of their fingers?

Rabbits can multiply, but only a snake can be an adder.

Where do tadpoles change into frogs?
In the croakroom.

What's yellow and smells of bananas?
Monkey sick.

If you catch a chinchilla in Chile,
And cut off its beard willy-nilly,
With a small razor blade,
You can say that you've made
A Chilean chinchilla's chin chilly.

What's a cat that has just swallowed a
    duck?
A duck-filled fatty-puss.

Ten cats were in a boat and one jumped
    out. How many were left?
None, because the others were copycats.

How do you get two elephants in a Mini?
One in the back and one in the front.

How do you get two hippos in a Mini?
*You can't. Two elephants are already
    there.*

A huge lion was roaring through the
jungle when he suddenly saw a tiny
mouse in his way. He stopped and snarled
at it menacingly.

'You're very small,' he growled fiercely.

'Well, I've been ill,' whispered the
mouse pathetically.

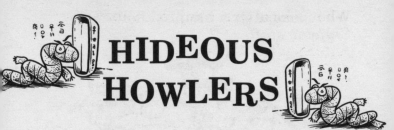

HIDEOUS HOWLERS

Why does a witch ride on a broom?
Because a vacuum cleaner is too heavy.

Did you hear about the undertaker who buried someone in the wrong place and got sacked for the grave mistake?

What do you call a dwarf novelist?
A short story writer.

What is a gargoyle?
What ghosts take for a sore throat.

What's a ghost's favourite dessert?
Strawberries and scream.

Why do mummies tell no secrets?
Because they keep everything under wraps.

Who looks after a haunted house?
Skeleton staff.

What's the perfect cure for dandruff?
Baldness.

Who serves spirits on an aeroplane?
The air ghostess.

Why do vampires brush their teeth?
To stop bat breath.

Why are vampires crazy?
Because they are often bats.

If a flying saucer is an aircraft, does that make a flying broomstick a witchcraft?

Where do werewolves send their laundry?
To the dry-screamers.

Where did the little witches go for their Christmas outing?
The phantomime.

What was the monster tortoise doing on the motorway?
About two hundred metres an hour.

Why did the little ghost keep looking in the mirror?
To make sure he was still not there.

What do witches like to read in the newspapers?
Their horrorscopes.

How many witches can you fit in an
empty coffin?
One – after that it isn't empty any more.

Where do ghosts go for their holidays?
The Isle of Fright.

Did you know that Count Dracula has a
new sign in the back window of his
carriage?
It says 'Give Blood Generously'.

Why does a witch ride a broomstick at
Hallowe'en?
So she can sweep the sky.

What day do ghosts prefer?
Moanday.

What do you have to do
to join Dracula's
fan club?
*Send off your name,
address and blood
group.*

Did you hear about the cannibal that only ate beans?
Human beans.

Why did the cannibal feel sick each time he ate a missionary?
Because you can't keep a good man down.

What happens when a witch loses her temper when riding a broomstick?
She flies off the handle.

What do you get when you cross a witch
with an iceberg?
A cold spell.

Why didn't the old skeleton want to go
the party?
His heart wasn't in it.

Who speaks at a ghosts' conference?
A spooksman.

Why are ghosts so bad at lying?
You can see right through them.

What do you get when a huge hairy
monster steps on Batman and Robin?
Flatman and Ribbon.

MADGE: Many years ago I had a close
encounter with a sub-human, alien
creature from outer space.
EMILY: Gosh! Did you report it to the
authorities?
MADGE: No, I married it.

What noise does a witch's breakfast cereal make?
Snap, cackle and pop!

FIRST WITCH: Goodness, your little girl's grown.
SECOND WITCH: Yes, she's really gruesome.

Why did the witch put her broom in the washing machine?
She wanted a clean sweep.

Why don't mummies catch cold?
They're always well wrapped up.

What happened when the abominable
   snowman bought a curry?
He melted.

Why did the skeleton run up the tree?
Because the dog was after his bones.

I have six legs, two bodies, fifteen eyes,
   four noses and twenty fingers on each
   hand. What am I?
Extremely ugly.

How does a ghoul start a letter?
'Tomb it may concern'.

What goes out at night and goes 'Chomp,
   suck . . . ouch!'
A vampire with fang-ache.

What sort of song does a ghost sing?
A haunting melody.

When do ghosts haunt skyscrapers?
When they are in high spirits.

What would you do if a monster broke in
  through your front door?
Run out through the back door.

What do you call a pretty, tidy, kind and
  considerate lady monster?
A complete failure.

FIRST VAMPIRE: A tramp stopped me in
  the street and said he hadn't had a bite
  for days.
SECOND VAMPIRE: What did you do?
FIRST VAMPIRE: I bit him.

What do cannibals do at a wedding?
They toast the bride and groom.

Knock, knock.
Who's there?
Witches.
Witches who?
Witches the way to go home?

A witch doctor was called out to a jungle village because a man was very ill. He examined the man carefully and, after much consideration, he said, 'I'll have to make you a special potion of bat's blood, crocodile skin, snake's tongue and ground insect wing.' So he went off to make the potion, brought it to the man and told him to drink it all right away.

Later that evening, he was called back to the village because the man wasn't any better. The witch doctor looked him over and said, 'Oh well then, you'd better take two aspirins every four hours.'

How can you tell if a giant is under your bed?
Your nose touches the ceiling.

A cannibal came home one night to find his wife chopping up a small native and a boa constrictor. 'Oh no, not snake and pygmy pie again!' he groaned.

What do vampires cross the sea in?
Blood vessels.

If you were surrounded by Dracula,
Frankenstein's monster, a werewolf
and a ghost, what would you be hoping?
That you were at a Hallowe'en party.

What does a monster eat after its tooth
has been taken out?
The dentist.

Where do ghosts like to swim?
In the Dead Sea.

What do you get if you cross Dracula with
Sir Lancelot?
A bite in shining armour.

What do ghosts like to ride at the
fairground?
The roller-ghoster.

What do you call an area where ghosts
live?
A terrortory.

What does a ghost rooster say?
Spook-a-doodle-do!

What was written on the metal monster's
 gravestone?
'Rust in Peace.'

Why do skeletons drink so much milk?
Because it's good for the bones.

LITTLE MONSTER: I've just bought a
 haunted bicycle.
LITTLE GHOST: How do you know it's
 haunted?
LITTLE MONSTER: There are spooks in the
 wheels.

Where do monsters study?
At ghoullege.

Why did the wizard put birdseed in his
shoes?
Because he had pigeon toes.

Why did the vicar put a fence around the
graveyard?
Because everyone was dying to get in.

Was Dracula ever married?
No, he was a bat-chiller.

Two young warlocks broke into a witch's
house on Hallowe'en night, thinking
she'd be out on her broomstick. As they
crept through the window they heard a
spooky voice screech, 'I'm going to start
by nibbling off your toes, then I'm going
to bite off your arms, and last of all I'm
going to chew your head . . .'

'Aargh!' screamed the warlocks, making
a mad dash back through the window and
getting stuck in the frame as they both
tried to get through at the same time.

'What was that noise?' asked the witch,
putting down her gingerbread man.

What do you get if you cross a ghost and a senior policeman?
A chief inspectre.

Why were the witches on strike?
They wanted sweeping reforms.

Where are famous monsters buried?
In Westmonster Abbey.

What do you call two witches who share a broomstick?
Broom-mates.

What do witches use pencil sharpeners for?
To keep their hats pointed.

What has fangs, is hairy and two metres tall?
A four-metre werewolf bending over to tie its shoelaces.

What do you get if you cross a mummy with a vampire?
A flying bandage.

What's big and green and sits in a corner
all day?
The Incredible Sulk.

Why do skeletons frighten easily.
Because they don't have any guts.

What do Dracula's children love to eat?
Fang-furters.

How do young spooks prefer their eggs?
Terrifried!

What sort of children does a monster
florist have?
Bloomin' idiots.

How do you disguise a mummy?
With masking tape.

Knock, knock.
Who's there?
Ivy.
Ivy who?
Ivy cast a spell on you.

A very ugly monstrosity
Wanted a look of ferocity,
With his nose in the air,
He walked like a bear,
Which only suggested pomposity.

What is a female monster's favourite
    saying?
'Demons are a ghoul's best friend.'

What do you get if you cross a monster
   with a cat?
A neighbourhood without dogs.

Why did the headless ghost go to the
   psychiatrist?
Because he wasn't all there.

How should you treat a sick monster?
With respect.

What do you call a monster who murders
   his father and mother?
An orphan.

How can you make a witch scratch?
Take away her W.

What did King Kong say when he heard
   his sister had a baby?
'Well – I'll be a monkey's uncle!'

Why did the zombie decide to stay in his
   coffin?
He felt rotten.

Two creatures from outer space landed by a traffic light.

'I saw her first,' said one of the creatures.

'So what?' said the other. 'I'm the one she winked at.'

What's Dracula's favourite chat-up line?
Hello gorgeous. What blood group are you?

FOUL FOOD

What flies and wobbles?
A jellycopter.

What has knobs on and wobbles?
Jellyvision.

MAN: This sponge cake is a bit tough.
WOMAN: It shouldn't be. I bought the
  sponge fresh from the chemist this
  morning.

What's green, covered in custard and
  miserable?
Apple grumble.

The sausage is a cunning bird,
With feathers long and wavy,
It swims about the frying pan,
And makes its nest in gravy.

What's worse than finding a maggot in an apple?
Only finding half a maggot.

What do you get if you cross a jelly with a sheepdog?
Collie wobbles.

What do you call a rude cabbage?
A fresh vegetable.

What cake wanted to rule the world?
Attila the Bun.

Waiter, there's a bug in my soup!
That's strange, it's usually a fly.

Waiter, there's a dead fly in my soup.
Yes sir, it's the heat that kills them.

When is food rude?
When it's got sauce.

Can an orange box?
No, but a tomato can.

Waiter, there's a button in my potato.
Well, you did ask for a jacket potato, sir.

Waiter, this stew isn't fit for a pig.
*Sorry, sir. I'll take it away and find you
some that is.*

Waiter, this lemonade is cloudy.
No, sir, it's the glass that's dirty.

Waiter, have you smoked salmon?
No, madam, I've only ever smoked a pipe.

Why are dumplings so unlucky?
They're always in a stew.

What's the best way to catch a fish?
Get someone to throw it at you.

Why did the baby strawberry cry?
His mother was in a jam.

What vegetables are found in boats?
Leeks.

Waiter, there's a frog in my soup!
That's right, sir. The flies are on holiday.

Waiter, there's a fly in my butter!
No, there isn't!
I tell you there's a fly in my butter!
And I tell you there isn't – it isn't a fly,
   it's a moth, and it isn't butter, it's
   marge – so there!

When are school dinners noisy?
When they're bangers and mash.

Why did the custard cry?
Because it saw the apple crumble.

Did you hear the one about the cornflake?
Well, I'll tell you next week – it's a cereal.

Did you hear about the two prunes that
    were arrested for being stewed?
They were remanded in custardy.

Did you hear about the orange that got
    stuck on the road?
It had run out of juice.

Waiter, you've got your big greasy thumb
    in my steak.
*I know, sir, but you wouldn't want it to
    fall on the floor again, would you?*

Waiter, I can't eat this soup.
I'm sorry, sir, I'll get the manager.
Manager, I can't eat this soup.
I'm sorry, sir. I'll call the chef.
Chef, I can't eat this soup.
Why not, sir?
I haven't got a spoon!

What kind of crisps fly?
Plane crisps.

Waiter, there's only one piece of meat
    here.
Sorry, sir. I'll cut it in two for you.

What do you call a train loaded with
    toffee?
A chew-chew train.

What car is like a sausage?
An old banger.

What do you call a lady who doesn't like
    butter?
Marge.

Waiter, this bread's got sand in it.
That's to stop the butter slipping off, sir.

How do you make an apple puff?
Chase it around the garden.

Which side of the apple is the left side?
The one that hasn't been eaten.

Why is a banana skin like a pullover?
Because it's easy to slip on.

What can a whole orange do but half an
    orange can't?
Look round.

Waiter, this tea tastes like dishwater.
Drink dishwater often, do we, sir?

What's the best butter in the world?
A goat.

Waiter, is there soup on the menu?
No, sir, I've wiped it off.

Waiter, what's this in my soup?
*I don't know, sir, all these insects look the
    same to me.*

What fills a field with music?
Popcorn.

What do scientists eat?
Microchips.

Which rich Arab invented flavoured
    crisps?
Sultan Vinegar.

A man saw a gardener pushing a
wheelbarrow filled with manure.
    'Where are you going with that?' he
asked.
    'I'm going to put it on my rhubarb,'
said the gardener.
    'Suit yourself,' said the man. 'But I put
custard on mine.'

What did Batman give Robin for
    breakfast?
Worms.

Knock, knock.
Who's there?
Lettuce.
Lettuce who?
Lettuce in, won't you?

Waiter, do I have to sit here until I die of
    starvation?
No, sir, we close at seven.

Waiter, there's a twig in my soup.
*Hold on, sir, and I'll call the branch
    manager.*

Waiter, this plate is wet.
That's your soup, sir.

Waiter, I'll have an egg. No, make that a
    steak.
I'm a waiter, sir, not a magician.

What nuts can be found in space?
Astronuts.

What did the chocolate say to the lollipop?
Hello, sucker.

CUSTOMER: I want a quick snack.
WAITER: How about runner beans?

What's the difference between a shark
  and spaghetti?
A shark won't slip off the end of your fork.

What's served in glasses and difficult to
  swallow?
A stiff drink.

Knock, knock.
Who's there?
Rosa.
Rosa who?
Rosa carrots grow in our garden.

Knock, knock.
Who's there?
Theresa.
Theresa who?
Theresa fly in my soup.

Knock, knock.
Who's there?
Diana.
Diana who?
*Diana thirst, can I have some water
   please?*

What's cowardly, thin and full of noodles?
Chicken soup.

Knock, knock.
Who's there?
Butter.
Butter who?
*Butter be quick, I have to go to the
   bathroom.*

Knock, knock.
Who's there?
Pizza.
Pizza who?
Pizza cake would be great right now.

What made the wine box?
It saw the rum punch.

How do you make a Swiss roll?
Lie him on his side and push him down a hill.

Knock, knock.
Who's there?
Hammond.
Hammond who?
Hammond eggs.

Knock, knock.
Who's there?
Sid.
Sid who?
Sid down and I'll make you a cup of tea.

What did the cat say to the mouse?
Pleased to eat you.

What did the first egg say to the second egg?
Heard any good yolks recently?

MOULDY MEDICINE

What happens if you eat Christmas decorations?
You get tinselitis.

How long should a dentist practise?
Until he gets it right.

Why did the man hit the dentist?
Because he got on his nerves.

PATIENT: Tell me the truth, doctor. Is it serious?
DOCTOR: Well, I wouldn't start watching any new serials if I was you.

PATIENT: Doctor, why are you writing on my toes?
DOCTOR: I'm just adding a footnote.

Doctor, doctor, I think I'm shrinking!
Well, you'll just have to be a little patient.

DOCTOR: You must take things quietly in future.
PATIENT: I do – I'm a cat burglar.

RECEPTIONIST: The new doctor's very funny. He'll have you in stitches.
PATIENT: I hope not, I've only come for a check-up.

PATIENT: Doctor, doctor, can you give me something for wind?
DOCTOR: Yes, here's a kite.

PATIENT: Well, doctor, how do I stand?
DOCTOR: I've no idea – it's a miracle.

Why do doctors and nurses wear masks?
So that if they make a mistake no one will know who it was.

Why did the nurse tiptoe past the medicine cabinet?
She didn't want to wake the sleeping pills.

Doctor Bell fell down the well,
And broke his collar-bone,
A doctor should attend the sick,
And leave the well alone!

DOCTOR: The best time to take a bath is just before retiring.
DAFT JACK: You mean I don't need another bath until I'm sixty-five?

MAN: Will I be able to read when I get my glasses?
OPTICIAN: Yes, sir.
MAN: That's good. I didn't know how to before.

Did you hear about the dentist who became a brain surgeon when his drill slipped?

When is an operation funny?
When it leaves the patient in stitches.

How do you stop a cold going to your chest?
Tie a knot in your neck.

Did you hear about the sick gnome?
He went to the elf centre.

Doctor, I've got double vision. How can I
  cure it?
Go around with one eye shut.

Knock, knock.
Who's there?
Jessica.
Jessica who?
Jessica than I thought, I'll get a doctor.

Knock, knock.
Who's there?
Sarah.
Sarah who?
Sarah doctor in the house?

Knock, knock.
Who's there?
Atch.
Atch who?
Nasty cold you've got.

Knock, knock.
Who's there?
Colin.
Colin who?
Colin the doctor, I'm not well.

Doctor, I feel like a pin.
I see your point.

Doctor, every night I dream there are
horrible green monsters under my bed.
What should I do?
Saw the legs off your bed.

Doctor, doctor, my child has just fallen
down a well.
You should get a book on raising children.

DOCTOR: You must take four teaspoonfuls
of this medicine before every meal.
PATIENT: But I've only got three
teaspoons.

BERT: My doctor's told me to give up golf.

SAM: Why, because of your health?

BERT: No, he looked at my score-card.

DOCTOR: Your system needs toning up. You should take a nice, cold bath every morning.

PATIENT: I do.

DOCTOR: You do?

PATIENT: Yes, I take a nice, cold bath and I fill it with nice, warm water.

Doctor, I feel like a yo-yo.
Sit down . . . sit down . . . sit down.

PATIENT: Doctor, I swallowed a clock last week.

DOCTOR: That could be serious! Why didn't you come to see me last week?

PATIENT: I didn't want to alarm anyone.

Why was the unemployed doctor angry?
Because he had no patients.

DOCTOR: How is your husband's rheumatism?

PATIENT'S WIFE: Not too good. I rubbed his back with brandy, as you suggested, and he broke his neck trying to lick it off.

PATIENT: Doctor, those strength pills you gave me aren't doing me any good at all.

DOCTOR: Why not?

PATIENT: I can't unscrew the bottle top.

What do you call a doctor who's butter-fingered?

A medicine dropper.

PATIENT: Doctor, I think I'm really ill.

DOCTOR: What are the symptoms? Do you have spots?

PATIENT: Yes, all over.

DOCTOR: Do your eyes ache?

PATIENT: Oh, yes. And my ears!

DOCTOR: And your colour's not too good, is it?

PATIENT: No.

DOCTOR: I'm exactly the same. I wonder what we've got.

REVOLTING RHYMES

There was an old man in a hearse,
Who murmured, 'Things might be worse.
Of course the expense,
Is simply immense,
But it doesn't come out of my purse!'

The rain makes all things beautiful,
The grass and flowers too.
If rain makes all things beautiful,
Why doesn't it rain on you?

There was an old man from Carlisle,
Who sat down one day on a stile.
The paint was still wet,
So he's sitting there yet,
But he hopes to get free with a file.

There was an old man from Penzance,
Who always wore sheet-iron pants.
He said 'Some years back,
I sat on a tack,
And I'll never again take a chance.'

There was a young boy called Edgar,
Who's learning to strum a guitar.
He practises long,
To learn a new song,
But knows just the chorus so far.

I'd like to have your picture,
It would be very nice,
I'd put it in the cellar,
To frighten all the mice.

I sat next to a duchess at tea,
And just as I feared it would be:
Her rumbling abdominal,
Was simply phenomenal,
And everyone thought it was me.

There was a young lady from Surrey,
Who cooked up a large pot of curry.
She ate the whole lot,
Straight from the pot,
And dashed to the loo in a hurry.

Poor old teacher, we missed you so,
When into hospital you had to go.
For you to remain there will be a sin,
We're sorry about the banana skin.

Little Miss Muffet,
Sat on her tuffet,
Eating chicken and chips.
Her sister, who's hateful,
Knicked half a plateful,
And strolled away licking her lips.

Hey diddle diddle,
The cat did a widdle,
Right in the middle of the floor.
The little dog laughed to see such fun,
And added a little bit more.

There was a young girl called Emma,
Who was seized with a terrible tremor.
She swallowed a spider,
Which wriggled inside her,
And left Emma in an awful dilemma.

There was a young man from Bengal,
Who went to a fancy dress ball.
He thought he would risk it,
And go as a biscuit,
But a dog ate him up in the hall.

A cannibal from Penzance,
Ate an uncle and two aunts,
A cow and a calf,
An ox and half,
And now he can't button his pants.

Mary had a parrot,
She killed it in a rage,
For every time her boyfriend came,
The damn thing told her age.

The wonderful wizard of Oz,
Retired from business becoz,
What with up-to-date science,
To most of his clients,
He soon was the wiz that woz.

There was a young man from Devizes,
Whose ears were of two different sizes.
The one that was small,
Was no use at all,
But his other one won several prizes.

Last night I killed my wife,
Stretched out on the parquet flooring.
I was loath to take her life,
But I had to stop her snoring.

There was a phantom named Pete,
Who would never play, drink or eat.
He said, 'I don't care
For tea or éclair.
Can't you see that I'm dead on my feet?'

There was a young lady named Sue,
Who carried a frog in her shoe.
When asked to stop,
She replied with a hop,
'But I'm trying to get into *Who's Zoo*!'

There was a young man from Quebec,
Who wrapped both his legs around his
  neck.
But then he forgot,
How to untie the knot,
And now he's an absolute wreck.

There was a young fellow called Ted,
Who liked to eat custard in bed,
But one day it spilt,
All over his quilt,
So he ate up his bedclothes instead!

Little Miss Muffet,
Sat on her tuffet,
Eating a bowl of stew.
Along came a spider,
And sat down beside her,
So she ate him up too.

An oyster from Kalamazoo,
Confessed he was feeling quite blue.
'For,' he said, 'as a rule,
When the weather turns cool,
I invariably get in a stew.'

There was an old man with a beard,
Who said, 'It's just as I feared:
Two owls and a hen,
Four larks and a wren,
Have all built their nests in my beard.'

There was an old man from Peru,
Who dreamt he was eating his shoe.
He awoke in the night,
In a terrible fright,
And found it was perfectly true!

Mary had a little lamb,
It ran around in hops.
It gambolled in the road one day,
And ended up as chops.

Sweet little Eileen Rose,
Was tired and sought repose,
But her big sister Claire,
Put a pin on her chair,
And sweet little Eileen rose.

There was an old farmer in Spain,
Who misguidedly prayed for rain.
The resultant showers,
Lasted for hours,
And washed his farm right down the
    drain.

Here I sit in the moonlight,
Abandoned by women and men,
Muttering over and over,
'I'll never eat garlic again!'

There was an old man called Morris,
Who had a wife called Doris.
Just as he feared,
She grew a beard,
So now he calls her Boris!

GROTTY GAGS

Why did the man cry out when he walked
into the bar?
Because it was an iron bar.

Where did Sir Lancelot study?
In knight school.

GIRL: Why is your brother so small?
BOY: He's only my half-brother.

What do you get when you cross an ocean
with a comedian?
Waves of laughter.

What is there more of, the less you see?
Darkness.

What did they give the man who invented
door knockers.
The No Bell prize.

What is the most common illness in
    China?
Kung flu.

What is a falsehood?
A fake hat.

Why is it dangerous to read a first-aid book?
Because you'll meet with a chapter of accidents.

What goes through water and doesn't get wet?
A shaft of sunlight.

What lives under the sea and carries people?
An octobus.

DAD: My shaving brush is hard and sticky.
SON: It was OK when I painted my bike with it yesterday.

My mum is working for a good cause.
'Cause she needs the money.

Why is the letter S scary?
Because it makes cream scream.

What is the longest night of the year?
A fortnight.

What do jelly babies wear on their feet?
Gumboots.

What can travel around the world yet stay
in one corner?
A postage stamp.

What goes at 300 kph on a washing line?
Honda pants.

GUEST: What are your weekly rates?
HOTEL MANAGER: I don't know. Nobody's
ever stayed that long.

What do you call an American drawing?
A Yankee doodle.

Where do you find baby soldiers?
In the infantry.

BILLY: Mum, can I have another glass of
water?
MOTHER: Another? You've had three
already!
BILLY: I know, but my bedroom's on fire!

Who wrote jokes and never grew up?
Peter Pun.

CATHY: What do you give a man who has
everything?
AMANDA: My telephone number!

What is green, has two legs and a trunk?
A seasick tourist.

WOMAN: I don't like this photo, it doesn't
do me justice.
HUSBAND: It's mercy you want, not
justice!

How do you cut the sea in half?
With a sea-saw.

What do you call a woman with two
toilets?
Lulu.

What happened to the man who slept
with his head under his pillow?
*When he woke up he found the fairies had
taken all his teeth out.*

MAN (on doorstep): I'm collecting for the old folks' home.
LITTLE BOY: Hang on, I'll go and get my grandad.

TOM: My mum suffers from a nervous condition.
BILLY: What's that?
TOM: Every time she reads my school report she faints.

What do you call a judge who has no thumbs?
Justice Fingers!

Why did the boy take a car to school?
To drive the teacher up the wall.

BOB: What does the O mean in your homework jotter?
JIM: It's supposed to be the moon. The teacher ran out of stars.

What is a mermaid?
A deep-she fish.

FRED: What are you doing?
TOM: Writing a letter to my brother.
FRED: But you can't write.
TOM: So what? My brother can't read.

What turns everything back to front but doesn't move?
A mirror.

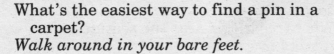

Keep Britain tidy – post your rubbish abroad!

What's the easiest way to find a pin in a carpet?
Walk around in your bare feet.

What's small, white and smells?
A pong-pong ball.

Where would you find a stupid shoplifter?
Squashed under the shop.

What did the Earl of York become when he received an OBE?
An Ear-l obe.

Why is the sky so high?
So the birds don't bump their heads.

What stars go to jail?
Shooting stars.

What's another name for a sugar daddy?
A lolly-pop.

What swings from a tree in a suit and tie?
A branch manager.

What tree grows near the seaside?
A beech tree.

What is another word for tears?
Glumdrops.

Why is life like a shower?
One wrong turn and you're in hot water.

JULIET: Romeo! Romeo! Wherefore art
 thou?
ROMEO: Down here in the flower bed – the
 trellis broke!

What travels faster, heat or cold?
Heat. You can catch cold.

What's greasy and makes you feel bad?
A chip on your shoulder.

What unlocks a Turkish house?
A turkey.

What did the letter say to the stamp?
'Stick with me and we'll go places.'

How many seconds in a year?
Twelve. January 2nd, February 2nd . . .

When is water not water?
When it's dripping.

What comes from trees and fights
   cavities?
A tooth pick.

When is longhand quicker than
   shorthand?
When it's on a clock.

Why are pianos so difficult to open?
All the keys are on the inside.

How do you get rid of a boomerang?
Throw it down a one-way street.

What kind of ears do engines have?
Engineers.

Who invented the first plane that couldn't
    fly?
The Wrong brothers.

PILOT: Mayday! Mayday!
CONTROL TOWER: Please state your height
    and position.
PILOT: I'm about one metre eighty and
    I'm sitting in the cockpit.

Knock, knock.
Who's there?
Adolf.
Adolf who?
*Adolf ball hit my dose, dat's why I talk dis
    way.*

FATHER: How are your exam marks, son?
BOY: They're under water.
FATHER: What do you mean?
BOY: Below C level.

Why did the farmer plough his field with
   a steamroller?
He wanted to grow mashed potatoes.

What do invisible babies drink?
Evaporated milk.

What's brown and prickly and squirts jam at you?
A hedgehog eating a doughnut.

What's clever, sweet and travels by Underground?
A tube of Smarties.

Why did Daft Jack wear all his clothes to paint his house?
Because the instructions said 'Put on at least three coats.'

What tools do you use in arithmetic?
Multipliers.

What did the dirt say to the rain?
'If this keeps up, my name will be mud.'

Why did the bald man go outside?
To get some freshair.

Why are brides unlucky?
They never marry the best man.

Three men were marooned on a desert island and were granted a wish each.

Two of the men wished to be back at home with their families, but the third man thought about his wish. Finally he said, 'I'm lonely. I wish my friends were here with me.'

Knock, knock.
Who's there?
N.E.
N.E. who?
N.E. body you like, so long as you let me in.

Knock, knock.
Who's there?
Laurie.
Laurie who?
Laurie driver.

Did you hear about the man who crossed an electric blanket with a toaster?
He kept popping out of bed all night.

What is green and brown and if it fell out
    of a tree would kill you?
A snooker table.

What spy hangs around department
    stores?
A counter spy.

POLICEMAN: Haven't I seen your face somewhere before?
CROOK: No, officer. It's always been here, right between my ears.

Knock, knock.
Who's there.
Dishes.
Dishes who?
Dishes your friend, open the door.

What happened to the author that died?
He became a ghost writer.

Where do zombies go for their jokes?
To crypt writers.

Why do ghosts like to haunt tall buildings?
Because there are lots of scarecases.

What do you use to flatten a ghost?
A spirit level.

MOTHER: How was your first day at school, Sam?

SAM: OK, except for a bloke called Sir, who kept spoiling all the fun.

What did the carpet say to the desk?
I can see your drawers.

MAD SCIENTIST: We're going to send this rocket up to the sun.

JOURNALIST: Won't it burn up?

MAD SCIENTIST: No, we're sending it at night.

What's always flying and never goes anywhere?
A flag.

What relation is a doorstep to a doormat?
A stepfarther.

What did the toothpaste say to the brush?
Give me a squeeze and I'll meet you outside the tube.

Knock, knock.
Who's there?
Little boy.
Little boy who?
Little boy who can't reach the doorbell.

What's an elastic-band thief called?
A rubber bandit.

What's it like being a dog?
Ruff!

Knock knock.
Who's there?
Gladys.
Gladys who?
Gladys the weekend, aren't you?

What does a giant parrot say?
*'Pretty Polly wants some seed –
    PRONTO!'*

Knock, knock.
Who's there?
Doughnut.
Doughnut who?
Doughnut take so long to answer the door again.

Why are porpoises so clever?
They swim around in schools.